Gymnastics Drills And Conditioning Exercises

By Karen M. Goeller

Gymnastics Drills and Conditioning Exercises
By Karen M. Goeller

Copyright © 2011 Goeller
All Rights Reserved.
Gymnastics Stuff, NJ

First edition was published in 2001.

ISBN: 978-1-4583-7621-3

www.GymnasticsBooks.com
www.KarenGoeller.com

Gymnastics Drills and Conditioning Exercises

"I have several of Karen's books, and I use them constantly. Each book contains such a wide variety of drills that I can pick and choose the ones that are best for my gymnasts. FABULOUS BOOKS!"
Moselle Campbell

"Full of information. While there were some things I already knew, there were other's that seemed helpful."
Amy Mckell

"In Gymnastics Drills and Conditioning Exercises, author and gymnast coach Karen M. Goeller can have you tumbling your way to the gold in no time." Cary Allman

FANTASTIC! A goldmine for new team & pre-team coaches. High quality, useful, and reasonably priced."
Sarah Jane Clifford, GTC, NY (Nat'l TOPS Testing Host)

"WONDERFUL book--packed with information. Super tool for visual learners. THANKS!"
M. Maxwell RI

"Super book, recommending to all my friends, fast delivery, helpful exercises!"
N Stevens-Brown, CA (American Vaulting Assoc. Coach)

"Great book! My daughter loves it. A#1 seller. Would recommend to all!!!"
D. Conine, OH

"It is a sum up of success on gymnastics. Let the words of New Generation exist with the day in this book"
Meng Kui Wang 40+ yrs in gymnastics, Men's Judge, Author, National Recruiter for China

"I received the book today and I am extremely pleased. Thanks so much for a great deal. "
L Robbins, VA

"The explanations were clear and the pictures helped."
M Soto, NY

"Your writing on gymnastics education is very good."
P Spadaro, NY USAG Chairman & VP USAIGC

"I Bring mine to the gym everyday!"
C Brouns, MA YMCA

"The exercises look great"(Sells book at camp store)
M Jacobsen, Owner USGTC

"Well written, easy to read, good conditioning ideas. Thanks!"
J Wisley, WA

"Great product! My daughter loves it!!"
M Mackins, NY

"Thanks for the book, its perfect."
J. Latshaw, NJ

Gymnastics Drills and Conditioning Exercises

This book includes drills and strength exercises that Karen has assigned to her gymnasts for many years. Although the drills, when done correctly have proven challenging to gymnasts of all levels, they are most useful to your developing gymnasts in USAG levels one through eight.

Positive feedback on this and my other books has come from many people, including Paul Spadaro who is the USAG NYS Chairman and USAIGC Vice President and the owner of the gymnastics camp USGTC. I knew that many people appreciated my work, but when I saw Bela Karolyi at Olympic Trials and he told me to keep up all the great work, I was truly thrilled. The most famous coach in the world validated my work after I've been such a fan of his for so many years.

I have spent thousands of hours coaching and I have educated thousands in the gymnastics and fitness communities with her books, training programs, articles, and in person.

It was a privilege to have worked at Karolyi's Gymnastics Camp in Texas for seven summers and to be one of his camp directors. I also worked at US Gymnastics Training Camp and International Gymnastics Camp for a decade of Holiday Clinics. Working at these camps along with working for Paul Spadaro and attending many USA Gymnastics events such as Regional Congress and the National TOPS Training Camp have all been contributing factors to my vast knowledge of the sport. I have always appreciated those who were so generous with their knowledge. When I published this book, I thought it was the perfect time to pass on my knowledge.

www.GymnasticsDrills.com
www.GymnasticsBooks.com
www.KarenGoeller.com

Table of Contents

RUNNING DRILLS FOR VAULT AND TUMBLING 1

Arm Swing

1. Have your athlete kneel or stand.
2. Have your athlete lift one arm to a forward middle position. Their elbow should be the same height as their shoulder.
3. Next have them bend that arm so that their fingers are pointing toward the ceiling. The bend should be 90 degrees.
4. Once they have the first arm position correct, have them lift the opposite arm behind them so that their elbow is as close to shoulder height as possible. Once that arm is lifted, have them bend it to a 90 degree angle as well. Their fingers may be at hip height.
5. Once they can form those shapes with their arms, have them swing\switch their arms so that the opposite arm is in front.
6. Have your athlete continue the arm motion for the run until they can perform it rapidly.

They will need this arm swing for their run.

Lunge Walks & Exploding Lunges

1. Take a large step with right foot. Make sure your athlete's toes are facing forward.
2. Keeping left foot behind, lower left knee toward floor, keeping chest upright.
3. Do not allow athlete to hit their back knee on the floor when approaching the low lunge position.
4. Front knee must be in line with front toe, not leaning in or out during entire exercise.
5. Front knee must not pass front toe. This is more an up and down motion rather than a forward movement exercise.
6. Left arm swings forward; left elbow should be almost even with shoulder and bent at a 90 degree angle.
7. Right arm swings back; right elbow as high as possible and bent at a 90 degree angle.
8. Stand and simultaneously repeat steps 1-4 with opposite leg and arm.
9. Athlete should stand up as tall as possible while stepping forward to next low lunge.
10. **Once mastered**, have your athlete perform an **explosive jump** from their knees and switch legs in the air between every few Lunge Walks. Have them lowerdown to the lunge (knees at 90 degree angle) position.

1 - 6   7

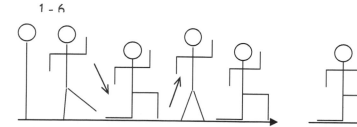

Notes

RUNNING DRILLS FOR VAULT AND TUMBLING 2

Knee Lift (High Knees)

1. **With a** Marching Motion **step** forward with the right leg and then immediately lift the left knee to hip height and the left foot to the height of the right knee.
2. Simultaneously lift the right arm forward so that the elbow is shoulder height and the fingers are facing the ceiling.
3. Lift the left elbow up and back. Both arms should remain bent with a 90 degree angle and should swing **alternately throughout the exercise.**
4. Once the Marching Knee Lift is mastered, perform the exercise with a **Running Motion.**
5. Swing left arm back, keeping the elbow bent and 90 degrees; using a running motion
6. Swing legs and arms rapidly, but travel forward slowly in order to focus on the actual knee lift with each step.

Kick Butt (Heel Lift)

1. With a **Walking Motion** step forward with the right leg and then immediately lift left heel up to touch buttocks.
2. Simultaneously lift the left arm forward so that the elbow is shoulder height and the fingers are facing the ceiling.
3. Lift the right elbow up and back. Both arms should remain bent with a 90 degree angle and should swing **alternately throughout the exercise.**
4. Simultaneously switch legs and arms, kicking buttocks with right heel and swinging right arm forward.
5. Once the Walking Butt Kick is mastered, perform the exercise with a **Running Motion.**
6. Swing legs and arms rapidly, but travel forward slowly in order to focus on the actual heel lift with each step.

Notes

RUNNING DRILLS FOR VAULT AND TUMBLING 3

Power Skips (Skipping with Explosive Movements for Height)

1. Step with left leg, immediately and aggressively bring right knee up and right toe next to the left knee.
2. As the knee and toe are being lifted, perform a hop with the supporting leg.
3. Just as aggressively, lift the left arm up and forward to initiate the arm swing, using the opposite arms as the legs.
4. In between each power skip, take two steps in order to focus on one leg at a time.
5. Have your athletes try this exercise backwards. Be careful not to let them trip over anything or bump into anything.

One Legged Lifts and Skips

1. With a Marching Motion step forward with the right leg and then immediately lift the left knee to hip height and the left foot to the height of the right knee. At the top of the lift, rise up on the toes\ball of supporting foot.
2. Simultaneously lift the right arm forward so that the elbow is shoulder height and the fingers are facing the ceiling.
3. The left elbow should be lifted up and back. Both arms should remain bent with a 90 degree angle and swing alternately throughout the exercise.
4. Once the knee lift is at it's highest point, return the foot to the floor (step forward onto that foot) and take another step forward in order to repeat the knee lift using the same knee down the entire runway .
5. Once one side\leg is learned, perform the exercise using the other side\leg the next time.
6. Once the one Legged Lift is mastered, perform the exercise with a **Hopping/Skipping Motion** on the supporting leg and swing the arms as if running.
7. Swing legs and arms rapidly and explosively for the skips.

1-5 ... Walks

6 - 7 ... Skips

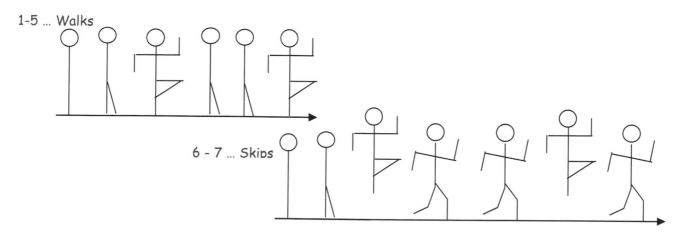

Notes

RUNNING DRILLS FOR VAULT AND TUMBLING 4

Deer Runs

1. With a leaping motion rapidly and agressively lift the right knee to hip height while simultaneously kicking the left leg back and up to buttocks height.
2. Once the right foot touches the floor immediately lift the left knee to hip height and kick the right leg back and up to buttocks height.
3. Continue traveling forward, rebounding from foot to foot.
4. Continue leaping from foot to foot, each time lifting the front knee to hip height and back leg to buttocks height.
5. Arms swing alternately as if running and should remain bent with a 90 degree angle.

Accelerations

1. Perform the knee lift/high knees drill in place.
2. Start movement/run forward slowly for the first 4-6 steps.
3. Suddenly increase speed (accelerate to top speed) as quickly as possible.
4. Both arms should remain bent with a 90 degree angle and swing alternately throughout the exercise.
5. Arm speed should increase with leg speed.

Quick Feet

1. Perform the knee lift/high knees drill in place, but move feet\legs as rapidly as possible.
2. After the sixth or seventh step quickly initiate a sprint forward.
3. Accelerate to top speed as quickly as possible.
4. Both arms should remain bent with a 90 degree angle and swing alternately throughout the exercise.
5. The difference between this and the acceleration is that this drill calls for rapid movement from the start and the acceleration allows the athlete to pick up speed gradually.

Notes

RUNNING DRILLS FOR VAULT AND TUMBLING 5

Sprint

1. Use either a vault runway or the diagonal of a floor exercise area.
2. The diagonal of floor exercise is recommended for higher safety regarding shock absorption.
3. If you use the vault runway, you should run past the vault rather than stopping in front of it.
4. Run at top speed down the runway past the vault or other marker appropriate for your sport.
5. With each step, lift the knees high, kick the buttocks, and swing the arms alternately.
6. Make sure the toes are facing forward with each step.
7. Continue to monitor technique.

Once good technique is established in the sprint the athlete can perform a variety of skills.

For Tumbling
1. Use the floor exercise diagonal or a tumbling strip.
2. Have the athlete sprint and perform a cartwheel or roundoff without slowing down before the skill.
3. A coach should be ready to spot because the speed of the run should produce a faster roundoff.

For Vaulting
1. Place a springboard on the runway or the floor exercise diagonal approximately $\frac{3}{4}$ of the way from the starting point.
2. Sprint with good technique down the runway and over the springboard at top speed as if it is not there. Do not stop, slow down, or jump on the board. Run right over the board.
3. Once comfortable sprinting over the board at top speed as if the board is not there place a soft landing mat at the high end of the board the long way.
4. Make sure it is a very large mat, especially if not using a floor exercise area.
5. Sprint with good technique, hurdle, and perform a straight jump using the springboard and landing on the soft mat. A coach should be standing at the mat and ready to spot because the speed of the run will propel the athlete higher and further than expected if all is performed correctly.
6. Many gymnasts do not already run at top speed for a straight jump.
7. Once comfortable running at top speed, the skill performed off the springboard can vary.
8. Again, make sure a coach is at the landing area and ready to spot the skills and landings.
9. Both arms should remain bent with a 90 degree angle and swing alternately throughout the exercise.
10. Arm speed should increase with leg speed.

Notes

<u>RUNNING DRILLS FOR VAULT AND TUMBLING 6</u>

Hill Runs (For Speed)

1. Set up a Mega-Wedge at edge of the runway or floor exercise diagonal.
2. Place a stack of panel mats with the short side against the wedge.
3. Make sure the mats are the height of the higher end of the wedge.
4. The mats will serve as a starting point and mini runway to initiate the sprint down hill.
5. Sprint down the hill and continue at top speed the entire length of the runway.
6. The drop from the wedge to the floor will feel awkward the first few times. Be ready.
7. Arms swing alternately and remain bent with a 90 degree angle throughout the drill.
8. Arm speed should increase with leg speed.

Using the hill/gravity for sprints will help the muscles become more accustomed to reacting quicker, producing faster runs/sprints for vaulting and tumbling.

Hill Runs Over Springboard

1. Place a springboard about 15 feet away from wedge.
2. Perform sprint down hill and continue running over and past the spring board as if it is not there.
3. Continue running at top speed until end of runway or floor.
4. Next, add a very large soft landing mat at the high end of the board.
5. Run at top speed down hill and perfrom a straight jump on the board, using the correct arm technique and body position in air.
6. A coach should be standing at the mat and ready to spot because the speed of the run will propel the athlete much higher and further than expected if all is performed correctly.

Using the hill/gravity for sprints will help the muscles become more accustomed to reacting quicker, producing faster runs/sprints for vaulting and tumbling.

Notes

VAULTING DRILLS 1

Three Board Hurdle

This is an underarm swing/hurdle drill.

1. Line up 3 boards, making sure they are very close/touching each other.
2. Place an appropriate landing mat at end.
3. Have your athlete jump from board one, to two, to three quickly and then land and stick on the mat.
4. Make sure the arm swing is used, the buttocks is under, the chest is up, and the body is tight.
5. Make sure the arms move quickly from side-low position, forward-middle, to a forward-high position; using arms to lift body.

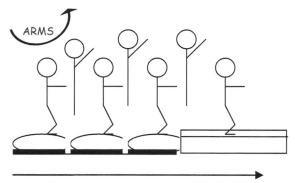

Handstand Hop/Block

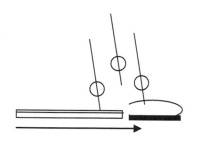

1. Place board in front of a low mat stack or landing mat.
2. Have your gymnast kick toward handstand placing their hands on board.
3. Tell them to immediately hop up to folded panel mats using a quick shrug motion/block of the shoulders.
4. Do not alow your athletes to arch their back. It can be very dangerous.
5. The more experienced gymnasts can also do this drill from a low mat up to the board for better shock absorption.

Handstand Hop/Block and Fall

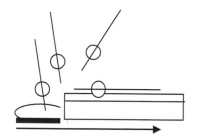

1. Place board in front of a very soft landing mat.
2. Have your gymnast kick toward handstand on board.
3. Tell them to immediately block/pop up to fall onto their back on very soft and slightly raised mat.
4. Make sure your gymnasts are hollow and very tight.

Handstand, Hop, Hop, and Fall

1. Have your gymnast kick toward a handstand on spring board and immediately block/pop up to the raised mat or wedge. (Handstand Hop)
2. Immediately after the Handstand Hop on raised mat, tell them to block/pop up to fall onto their back on very soft and slightly raised mat.
3. Remind your gymnast to keep their stomach tight in order to prevent injury.

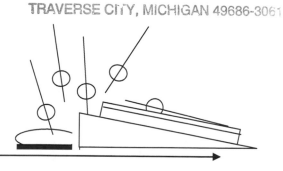

<u>Notes</u>

VAULTING DRILLS 2

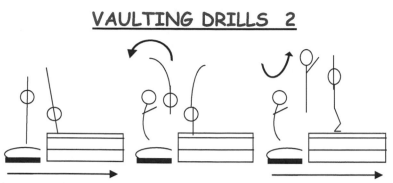

Snap Down to Bounce Up

1.   Place a mat stack the long way (as if an extension of the board) in front of a spring board.
2.   Have your gymnast kick to brief handstand on mats.
3.   Instruct them to snap their buttocks under and lift their chest to land on feet on the board.
4.   Focus on the tight positions, buttocks under, and arm lift.
5.   As soon as their feet touch the board, your gymnast must arm-circle forward and up (arm lift) for a straight jump up to the mat stack.
6.   Your gymnast must land on the mat stack with their knees slightly bent, arms up, buttocks under, and chest up.
7.   This is an arm lift and body position drill during the board phase of a vault.

Hop, Snap Down, Bounce Up

1.   Once Snap Down is mastered have your gymnast kick toward handstand placing their hands on board.
2.   Tell them to immediately hop up to folded panel mats onto their hands using a quick shrug motion/block of the shoulders.
3.   Next have them snap down/get their chest up to land on feet on the board.
4.   As soon as their feet touch the board, they must arm-circle forward and up for a straight jump up to the mat stack.
5.   Your gymnast must land on the mat stack with their knees slightly bent, arms up, buttocks under, and chest up.
6.   This is an arm lift and body position drill during the board phase of a vault.

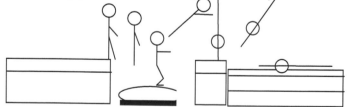

Drop and Pop (Handspring)

1.   Place a spring board between two spotting blocks or mat stacks.
2.   Place a longer mat stack with a very soft landing area at the end. (Level 4 Vault Resi.)
3.   Have your gymnast stand on spotting block that is closest to bottom of board.
4.   Then have them drop down to board then immediately hurdle, using the arm swing upward, and jump to handstand on mat stack.
5.   Once in the hands touch mat they must block/pop up to land on back on the soft mat.

Notes

VAULTING DRILLS 3

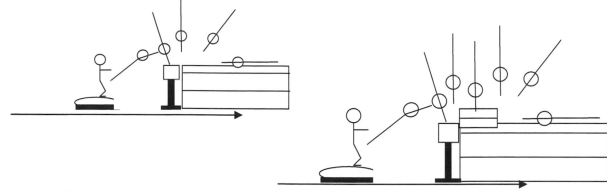

Handspring Block to Back

1. Set up a high mat stack behind the vault table or use the stack without the table for the less experienced gymnasts. Make sure the mat is very long.
2. Have your gymnast sprint toward the board and vault table.
3. Instruct them to jump on spring board, lifting their arms, keeping their buttocks under and chest up to perform the preflight phase of a handspring vault.
4. Once their hands touch the vault, instruct them to block/pop up off the vault to land on their back.
5. They must land on their back on a pit or soft stack of mats

Handspring, Block, Block

1. Raise the height of mats so they are 1-2" higher than the table.
6. Have your gymnast sprint toward the board and vault table.
7. Instruct them to jump on spring board, lifting their arms, keeping their buttocks under and chest up to perform the preflight phase of a handspring vault.
2. Once their hands touch the vault, instruct them to block/pop up off the vault up to the mat in a handstand position.
3. The athlete can then fall to their back on the mat.
4. When comfortable blocking and landing on the mat higher than the table instruct your gymnast to block/pop up to the mat that is higher than the table and then again block/pop to land on their back on the soft mat. (Hands touch vault, 1st mat, 2nd mat.)

Handspring to Feet on Stack

1. After the Handspring Hop, Hop is mastered, allow your gymnast to handspring to feet on a very stable and level mat stack.
2. Make sure your gymnast does not arch. If they are go back to the Handspring Hop drills landing on the back.

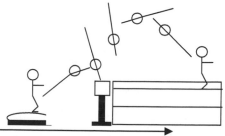

Notes

VAULTING DRILLS 4

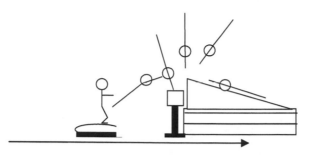

Handspring to Back on Wedge Mat

1. Set up a mat stack with a soft wedge mat on top. Place the higher end closer to the vault. Place mats on the floor below the wedge mat. A gymnast may slide down the mat id she is powerful.
2. Have your gymnast perform the Handstand Block (Handspring) to their back.
3. This should more closely simulate the Handspring positions because of the angle while continuing to work on blocking and body tightness.

Half-On and Miss Feet

1. Have your gymnast perform a Half-On Vault.
2. They must run at top speed/sprint toward the spring board and table.
3. Once they contact the spring board and jump up, have them half turn/twist before their hands contact the table.
4. They must block/pop up and lift their chest immediately by pushing down on table.
5. Your gymnast should feel and look like they are standing up in the air, facing the table.
6. The gymnast must continue to rise and then fall to their back on a very soft wedge mat, missing their feet and remaining tight.

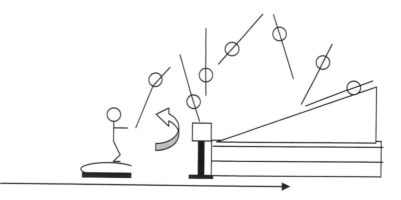

Notes

CONDITIONING AND DRILLS FOR BARS 1

Pull Ups & V Pull Ups

1. Have your gymnast hang from a bar with a straight body or with toes at bar height for the "V".
2. For the "V" Pull Up, the toes must face the ceiling throughout pull up and legs remain close to bar throughout the exercise. (Keep V shape).
3. Keeping hands slightly wider than shoulder width. Pull collar bones to bar and elbows to ribs.
4. Perform this exercise with palms facing in, using a narrower than shoulder grip and also with a mixed grip to strengthen a variety of areas.
5. The rings may also be used for pull ups.

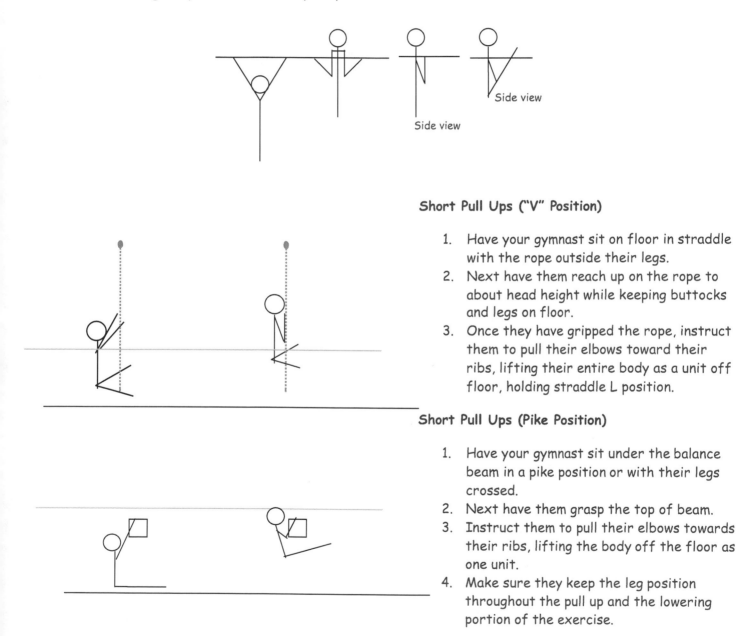

Short Pull Ups ("V" Position)

1. Have your gymnast sit on floor in straddle with the rope outside their legs.
2. Next have them reach up on the rope to about head height while keeping buttocks and legs on floor.
3. Once they have gripped the rope, instruct them to pull their elbows toward their ribs, lifting their entire body as a unit off floor, holding straddle L position.

Short Pull Ups (Pike Position)

1. Have your gymnast sit under the balance beam in a pike position or with their legs crossed.
2. Next have them grasp the top of beam.
3. Instruct them to pull their elbows towards their ribs, lifting the body off the floor as one unit.
4. Make sure they keep the leg position throughout the pull up and the lowering portion of the exercise.

Notes

CONDITIONING AND DRILLS FOR BARS 2

Bent Arm Levers

1. Have your gymnast hang from a bar. Be ready to spot them.
2. Instruct your gymnast to perform a pull up, collar bones to bar and elbows to ribs.
3. Next instruct your gymnast to lean back, straighten elbows, and simultaneously pull thighs to the bar. Their body must move as one tight, hollow unit.
4. Once your gymnast is hanging upside down with straight arms and their thighs on the bar, instruct them to pull their chin back toward the bar and lower legs to return to top of a pull up position.

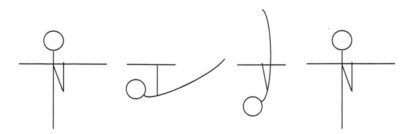

Straight Arm Levers

1. Have your gymnast hang from a bar.
2. Be ready to spot them.
3. Keeping their arms straight, instruct them to lift their toes towards the wall in front of them then toward the ceiling.
4. They must bring their thighs up to the bar.
5. Once upside down with their thighs on the bar, allow them to slowly lower their body to a straight hang position.

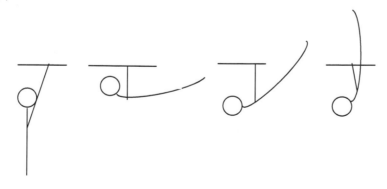

Notes

CONDITIONING AND DRILLS FOR BARS 3

Hollow Toes to Thighs

1. Have your gymnast hang from a bar. Be ready to spot them.
2. Next have them lift their ankles to the bar. ("Leg Lift")
3. Keeping their arms straight, instruct them to slide their legs up bar until their thighs are on bar and they are hanging upside down in a similar position to the top of the straight arm lever.
4. Next instruct them to slowly lower their buttocks, but keep their ankles on the bar.
5. Have them repeat several before stopping.

This drill is useful for glide kips and clear hip circles.

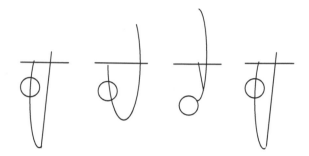

Modified Candlestick Pulls

1. Have your gymnast lie on their back holding the bar base or something very stable that will not fall on them.
2. Keeping their arms straight and hips open/straight, have them pull up to a near candlestick position.
3. Their toes should be above their hips not their head.
4. Once at the top of the modified candlestick, their toes should be pointed outward as if reaching for the crease between the ceiling and wall they can see, rather than straight up, as in the traditional candlestick position.
5. Instruct your gymnast to slowly lower their legs back to the starting position, lying flat on the floor.
6. Your gymnast's heels must reach the floor at the same time as their buttocks.
7. Be sure their entire body lifts and lowers as one unit. Your gymnast must remain tight in order for this drill to be performed correctly.

Notes

CONDITIONING AND DRILLS FOR BARS 4

Leg Lifts for Glide Kips

1. Place a block or mat stack beneath the low bar.
2. Have your gymnast lie on their back on the block, holding bar as if they just completed a glide.
3. Make sure they keep their arms straight, arms near their ears, their shoulders and hips open, buttocks under, and their legs straight.
4. Instruct them to keep their head off the block and between their ears.
5. Instruct your gymnast to quickly lift their toes/ankles towards bar.
6. Next have them slowly lower their legs back to the extended glide position and again quickly lift their legs, performing several repetitions.
7. Your gymnast must keep their buttocks under the entire time.

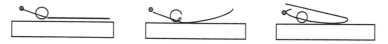

Glides

1. Have your gymnast stand slightly further than arms distance from low bar.
2. Instruct them to jump, immediately lift toes forward and tuck buttocks under while in air.
3. Once in air, they must grasp the bar, holding a hollow and slightly piked position.
4. Your gymnast must then glide forward, keeping their feet off the mat and reaching a completely extended position, similar to the starting position of the **Leg Lifts for Glide Kips**.
5. Either allow them to swing backward and connect as many glides as possible.
6. Or allow them to release the bar while extended to land on their feet on a mat on the opposite side of bar. Be ready to spot your gymnast.

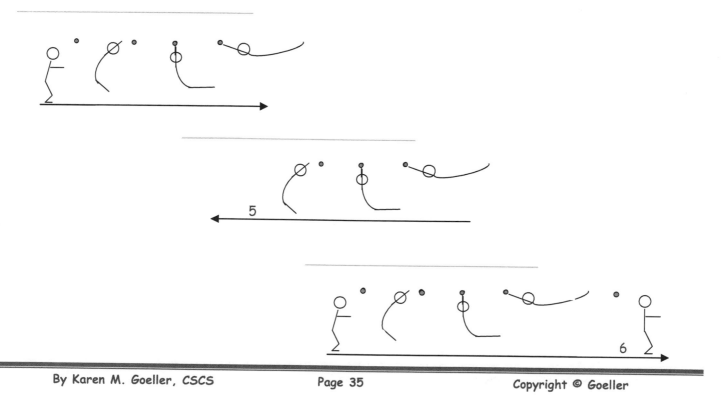

Notes

Glide and Toes to Bar

1. Have your gymnast stand slightly further than arms distance from low bar.
2. Instruct them to jump, immediately lift toes forward and tuck buttocks under while in air.
3. Your gymnast must immediately grasp bar, holding a hollow and slightly piked position.
4. Once on the bar, your gymnast must glide forward, keeping their feet off the mat and reaching an extended position.
5. Once they are extended, instruct them to bring their toes/ankles to bar and hold them on the bar, even when the body swings/falls (due to gravity) to the hanging position.

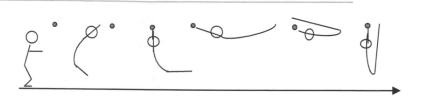

Octagon Glides & Toes To Bar

1. Have your gymnast grasp bar and place their feet on an octagon or barrel. Instruct them to hold a hollow and slightly piked position and to keep their buttocks under while gliding.
2. Once on the bar, your gymnast must glide forward and then roll backward, keeping their legs on the barrel/octagon for three full glides. (Your gymnast must reach an extended position each time.)
3. Once your gymnast is extended for the third time, instruct them to quickly bring their toes/ankles to bar and hold them on the bar, even when the body swings/falls (due to gravity) to the hanging position.

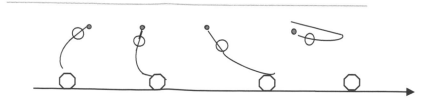

Notes

CONDITIONING AND DRILLS FOR BARS 6

Band Kips

1. Wrap a fitness band or surgical tubing around the base of very sturdy equipment such as the beam, vault, or bar base.
2. Instruct your gymnast to lie on their back and grasp the band or surgical tubing. Their head should be closer to the base than their feet.
3. Have your gymnast bend their knees.
4. Make sure your gymnast is holding the band very tight, while keeping their arms straight and close to their body.
5. Next instruct them to pull the band toward the ceiling and then down toward their thighs.
6. They may then return the band to the starting position slowly using the same direction, toward the ceiling then toward the base.
7. This should simulate the upper body while performing a **kip** on the bars.

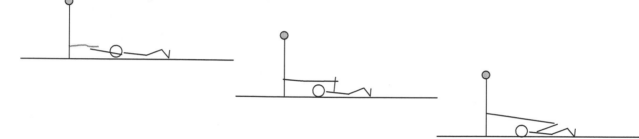

Band Casts

1. Wrap a fitness band or surgical tubing around the base of very sturdy equipment such as the beam, vault, or bar base.
2. Instruct your gymnast to lie on their back and grasp the band or surgical tubing. Their feet should be closer to the base than their head.
3. Have your gymnast bend their knees.
4. Make sure your gymnast is holding the band very tight, while keeping their arms straight and close to their body.
5. Next instruct them to pull the band toward the ceiling and then down toward their ears\head..
6. They may then return the band to the starting position by slowly using the same direction, toward the ceiling then down toward the base/thighs.
7. This should simulate the upper body while performing a **cast to handstand** on the bars.

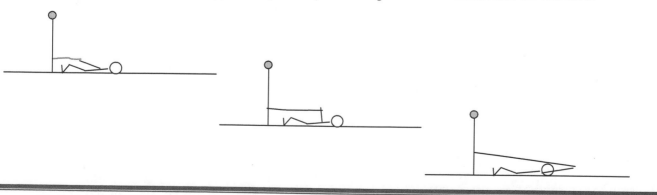

<u>Notes</u>

CONDITIONING AND DRILLS FOR BARS 7

P-Bar Walks

1. Set up either 2 stacks of panel mats or 2 blocks, leaving enough space to walk between.
2. Place a mat on the floor between the mat stacks.
3. Have your gymnast stand between the mat stacks.
4. Next instruct them to support themselves, one hand on each mat stack.
5. While supporting themselves, they must keep their feet off the floor, and may bend their knees if necessary,
6. Once they can support themselves in this position, **allow them to walk** forward with their hands\upper body supporting them to end of stack/block.
7. Once forward walking is performed, your gymnast should walk backwards.

P-Bar Swings
1. Once walking forward and backward is mastered, have your gymnast remain in the center of the stack supported on their hands with their feet off the floor.
2. Next have them (tap) **swing their lower body** (legs) forward and backward, keeping their arms straight and attempting to swing to a handstand at the top of backward swing.
3. Instruct your gymnast not to swing too high on the front swing. They can fall to the floor on their back easily.

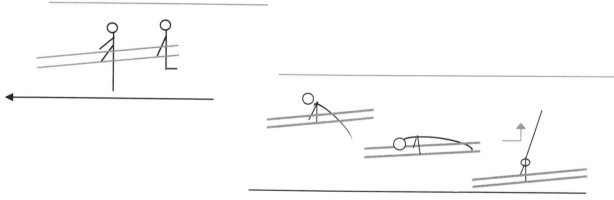

Octagon Rocks

1. Place an octagon\barrel in front of a floor bar.
2. Have your gymnast stand between the bar and octagon/barrel.
3. Instruct them to place their hands on the floor or bar and shins\ankles on the octagon\barrel.
4. While keeping their arms straight, body tight, hollow, and legs straight, instruct them to rock forward and backward.
5. They should rock from their ankles to their knees, without allowing their thighs to touch octagon.
6. Your gymnast should go from a stretched shoulder position to a planche position and then return to stretched shoulder position.

Notes

CONDITIONING AND DRILLS FOR BARS 8

Octagon Rock to Handstand

1. After the Octagon Rock is mastered, have your gymnast perform the octagon rock and hold the forward/planche position.
2. Once your gymnast can reach the planche position from the octagon rock comfortably, instruct them to lift one leg toward a hansdstand while keeping their shoulders forward.
3. Remind them to keep tight and their shoulders in the correct position to simulate shoulder movements for the cast handstand.
4. Some gymnasts are better able to reach the handstand if they perfrom this drill with quick movements.

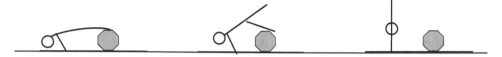

Bounce to Handstand

1. Place either a "Handstand Trainer" or a mini trampoline in front of a floor bar. The lower end should be closer to the bar than the higher end if using a mini trampoline.
2. Have your gymnast place their hands on the floor bar and their shins on the bungee or feet on the trampoline bed.
3. Instruct them to lift one leg and then quickly kick it down to jump start the bounce.
4. Once in the air, have your gymnast open their shoulders to perform a handstand and then planche to return to the starting position. The goal is to perform several repetitions with a tight and hollow body. Their shoulders should be forward (planche) when not in the actual handstand.
5. Instruct your gymnast to bounce, lifting and lowering their body as one unit.
6. Do not allow them to pike or opening at the top.
7. When done correctly, this should simulate a cast handstand.

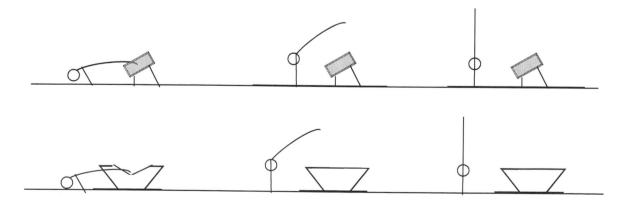

Notes

Presses on Block

1. Use a spotting block, a mat stack, or the balance beam.
2. Have your gymnast start in front support on block, mat stack, or beam.
3. Instruct them to slightly lean forward and slowly slide their legs up the block, mats, or beam until their ankles reach the top edge of the block, mat, or beam.
4. Once they are as high as they can go instruct them to slide back down to front support and repeat the press.
5. Or place their feet on top of block, mats, or beam to a standing or squatting position.
6. Or roll out of press onto block or mats if it is long enough.
7. Or press handstand out of press/slide up.

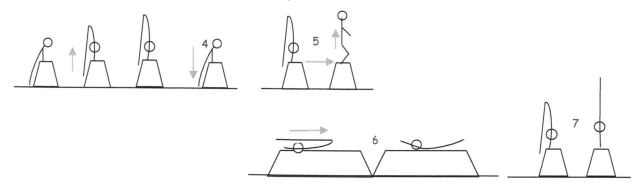

Cast & Hold

1. Be ready to spot.
2. Have your gymnast start in a front support on the bar.
3. Hold your gymnast's shoulders and shins to prevent them from falling.
4. Instruct them to cast: pike and lean forward, look at knees, and then quickly and immediately kick legs back, push hips off bar, and push down on bar with hands and upper body.
5. Gymnast must remain tight and hollow with their arms straight.
6. Make sure your gymnast does not lean too far forward. If they do, they may collapse.
7. Hold them in the horizontal position and help your gymnast rock forward and back as if performing the octagon rock drill, but this time it is on the bar.
8. Once your gymnast is able to remain tight while being held in the correct position as well as while rocking forward and back, you may be able to lift them up to a handstand position.
9. Return your gymnast back to the bar slowly and carefully in a support position.

Notes

CONDITIONING AND DRILLS FOR BARS 10

Wall Climbs

1. Have your gymnast stand with their back close to padded wall.
2. Instruct them to place hands on floor/mat approximately 2 feet from wall.
3. Next have them place their feet on the wall.
4. Once your gymnast is strong enough in that position...
5. Instruct them to simultaneously walk their hands in towards wall and feet up wall towards ceiling until their forehead touches wall and their shoulders touch their ears.
6. Keeping their arms straight, instruct them to *either* walk back out, remaining very tight.
7. *Or* keeping arms straight, allow them to roll out and slide their feet back down the wall.
8. **Once this is mastered,** have your gymnast perform shoulder shrugs in the handstand position before rolling or walking back out.
9. Take precautions...the mat must be secured against wall and the inexperienced gymnast must be spotted in order to prevent falling into arched position against wall.

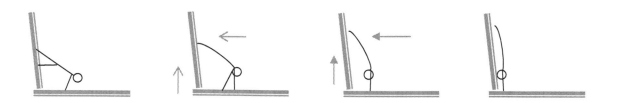

Back Extension to Climb

Once the Wall Climb and Roll Down are mastered.

1. Have your gymnast stand on a mat with their back facing a padded wall, approximately body-distance from the wall, including their arms.
2. Instruct them to perform a straight-arm back extension and aim their feet toward wall.
3. Once their feet reach the wall, instruct them to continue to walk in toward the wall, sliding their feet up the wall simultaneously.

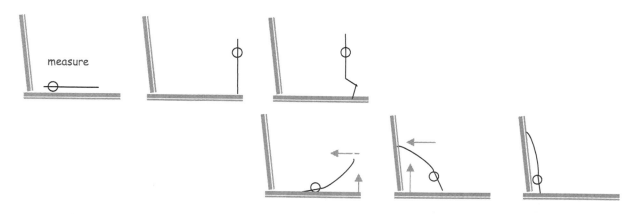

Notes

Straight Arm Cast/Lift Drill

1. Be ready to spot.
2. Instruct your gymnast to sit on the floor with their knees bent and back against a padded wall.
3. Have them hold a straight bar or two light dumbbells with their palms facing the floor.
4. Instruct them to raise their arms forward and upward simulating a cast to handstand on bars.
5. Once at the top, instruct your gymnast to lower the bar or dumbbells by bringing them forward and then to the low front position.
6. Make sure the keep their elbows nearly straight, but not locked on this drill.

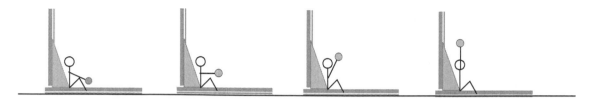

Lie Down Cast/Kip Drill (Very advanced version of Band Kips and Band Casts)

1. Be ready to spot.
2. Have your gymnast lie on their back between two folded panel mats.
3. Mats must be higher than your gymnast for safety reasons! (If the bar falls, it should land on the mats, not your gymnast.)
4. There should be room for the bar to touch floor after it is lifted over your gymnast's head for full range of motion. (cast handstand)
5. Instruct your gymnast to hold the straight bar (that is long enough to rest on both of the mats).
6. The bar can have weights, depending upon the strength and experience of the gymnast and coach.
7. Start with the bar at thigh level, resting on the mats. (to simulate a front support)
8. Your gymnast may need more spot on the initiation phase of the exercise than the return phase. Be prepared to spot all phases of this exercise.
9. Instruct your gymnast to keep their arms straight, but not to lock their elbows.
10. Next, instruct them to lift the bar up toward ceiling and then toward the floor above their head to simulate a cast to handstand motion with their upper body.
11. Instruct your gymnast to continue to hold the bar securely and then lift bar up toward ceiling again and lower to the mat right above their thighs to simulate a kip with their upper body.

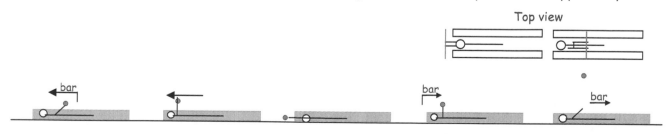

Notes

Clear Hip Body Shape Drill

1. Have your gymnast start in a front support position on the bar.
2. Be ready to spot.
3. Instruct them to perform a small cast.
4. As they pull back towards bar they should drop their shoulders back and down. Your gymnast will drop to the bottom half of a hip circle, but their thighs and hip should not touch the bar.
5. Their head should stay in. (Similar to a "hollow rock' position.)
6. Instruct them to remain tight and hollow and help them hold this position upside down with their thighs near the bar. (A front support upside down)
7. You can help your gymnast perfrom baby rocks as if they are going to complete the circle, all without their hips touching the bar. The purpose is to practice the round shape for clear hip circles.
8. Lift your gymnast by their shoulder to return them to a front support position.

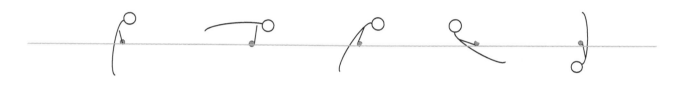

Block Clear Hip Drill

1. Have your gymnast stand on a block/mat stack holding the low bar.
2. Be ready to spot.
3. Instruct them to jump up and forward to reach a position as if they just performed a small cast.
4. Instruct them to immediately drop their shoulders back, keeping their head in and body hollow/tight, and then circle bar.
5. Your gymnast's legs should not touch the bar at any time throughout the circle around the bar.
6. When your gymnast can see the floor, instruct them to flick their wrists in order to get their hands on top of bar.
7. Once their hands are on top of the bar, tell them to push down with their arms, and raise their arms towards ears/open up the shoulder angle in order to land on the block again.
8. As your gymnast becomes more advanced, you may be able to raise the block in order to simulate a higher clear hip circle.

<u>Notes</u>

CONDITIONING AND DRILLS FOR BARS 13

Tap Drill

1. Have your gymnast hang from the bar.
2. Be ready to spot.
3. Instruct your gymnast to squeeze everything in their body tight.
4. Once they are tight, instruct them to stick their armpits out toward the wall they can see. This will cause them to become just slightly arched in their upper back. (Their toes should be slightly behind them.)
5. Next instruct them to pull their arm pits back in. They should pass through the straight position to a hollow position. At that point their toes should be slightly front of them.
6. Remind your gymnast to squeeze their buttocks the entire time. This exercise requires movement of the shoulders, not the lower back.
7. Repeat the positions using the shoulders to form the arch and hollow shapes necessary for tap swings, giants, and several other skills on bars.

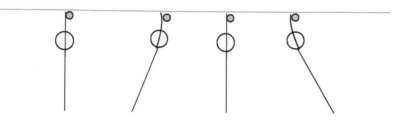

Tap Swing to Candlest

1. Have your gymnast perform 2-3 tight tap swings.
2. A coach must spot this drill.
3. At the top of the last swing instruct them to shape their body in a candlestick position.
4. Once shaped like a candlestick, instruct your gymnast to release bar and hold the candlestick shape in the air.
5. Either **hold your gymnast** in this position in air and slowly lower them to their feet.
6. Or place a **porta/resi pit** or very soft and high stack of mats to allow your gymnast to land on their back on the soft mat stack. A coach must be ready to spot.

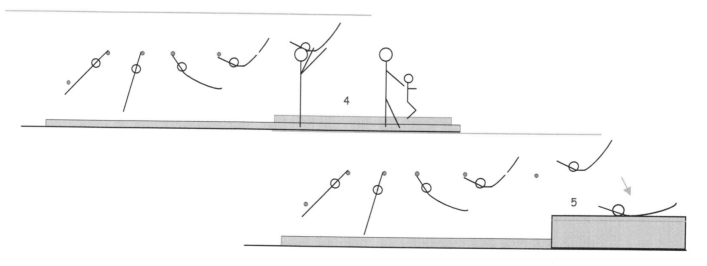

Notes

CONDITIONING AND DRILLS FOR BARS 14

Butt Swings (Forward & Backward)

1. Have your athlete start seated on the floor with their knees in a **tucked** position.
2. Instruct them to lift their feet off the floor, keeping the tucked position.
3. Next instruct them to place their hands on the floor beside their body, but reach forward.
4. Once they have reached forward, instruct them to shift their weight from their buttocks to their hands, lifting their buttocks off floor.
5. Once they have shifted their weight, have them swing their buttocks forward, passing their arms with their hips.
6. They should finish the exercise with their hands on the floor in back of their body.
7. Keeping their feet off the floor, your gymnast should repeat the exercise several times, down the vault runway, the floor exercise area, or a long strip of mats.
8. **Once your gymnast masters the Butt Swing Forward,** have them perform the same drill in reverse, traveling backwards.
9. **After your gymnast has mastered the tucked** butt swing, have them try it with straight knees, in a pike-V position.

Traveling forward will train the kip muscles and traveling backwards will train the cast muscles. Keeping their feet off the floor will train their hip flexors for the glide on bars.

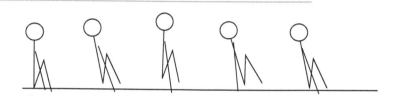

Straddle Butt Swings

1. This is the same drill as the "Butt Swings" above, but in a straddle position.
2. Make sure your athlete's hands remain in front them as they travel forward.
3. Once forward is mastered, have your athlete travel backward.
4. When your athlete's buttocks is lifted off the floor, their legs should also leave the floor.
5. Again, have them repeat the exercise down the vault runway, the floor exercise area, or a long strip of mats.

Traveling forward will train the kip muscles and traveling backwards will train the cast muscles. Keeping their legs up will train their hip flexors for the glide and straddle jumps on floor.

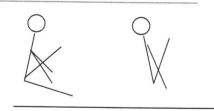

Notes

CONDITIONING AND DRILLS FOR BARS 15

Scooter Pulls/Pushes

1. Have your gymnast sit on their feet while kneeling on a flat board with wheels. (anything as low to ground as a skateboard)
2. Instruct your gymnast to reach forward placing both of their hands (palms or fingertips) on the floor with their fingers facing the direction they are traveling in.
3. Using their arms, have them pull their scooter forward while their hands appear to be pushing the floor back. This exercise should simulate the end of a glide kip on bars with their arms.
4. Once forward is mastered, have your gymnast perform this drill in reverse, traveling backwards. Backwards should simulate a cast on bars.
5. Instruct your gymnast to keep their hands away from the wheels.

Rainbow Walk (Pulls/Pushes)

1. Have your gymnast get in a long, round, support position shaped like a rainbow. They should be hollow and not have any shoulder or hip angles. Instruct them to squeeze their buttocks and remain that tight throughout the exercise.
2. Once in the correct position, have your gymnast walk using only their hands/arms and keeping their feet pointed.
3. They will literally drag their feet while each arm simulates the movement of a kip on bars.
4. Once your gymnast has mastered this Rainbow Walk forward, have them perform the drill traveling backwards. When they walk backwards, they should flex their feet. Backwards will simulate a cast on bars.
5. Have your gymnast repeat this exercise down the vault runway, the floor exercise area, or a long strip of mats.

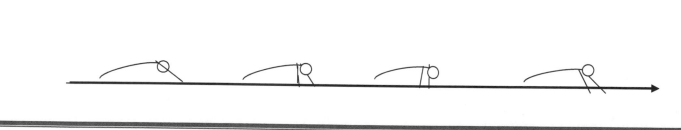

Notes

CONDITIONING AND DRILLS FOR DANCE 1

Hip Flexor Drills - Straddle

1. Have your athlete sit on floor in straddle position.
2. Instruct them to place their hands in front of their body on the floor slightly further than a natural/relaxed placement in order to force the athlete to lean forward.
3. Keeping their legs straight, feet pointed, and buttocks on floor, instruct your gymnast to lift both of their legs to shoulder height and then return to starting position.
4. Have your athlete repeat this exercise several times quickly.
5. As your athlete gains strength in their hip flexors, their hands can be placed further from their body.

Hip Flexor - Pike

1. Have your athlete sit on the floor in a pike position. (Legs straight out in front and together.)
2. Instruct them to place their hands on the floor next to their knees.
3. Keeping their legs straight, feet pointed, and their buttocks on the floor, instruct them to lift both of their legs to shoulder height and then return to the starting position.
4. Repeat several times quickly.
5. As your athlete gains strength in their hip flexors, their hands can be placed further from their body, closer to ankles.

Hip Flexor Drills with Added Lift.

1. Have your athlete sit on the floor in a straddle position.
2. Instruct them to place their hands in front of their body on the floor slightly further than a natural/relaxed placement in order to force the athlete to lean forward.
3. Have them lift one leg to shoulder height.
4. Instruct your athlete to keep that leg up and then lift their other leg to shoulder height.
5. Once their second leg is at shoulder height, instruct your athlete to lift both legs even higher. ("1, 2, both")
6. Make sure your athlete continues to lean forward throughout exercise and keep excellent form.

In fond and loving memory of Renville Duncan, Our Choreographer and so much more...

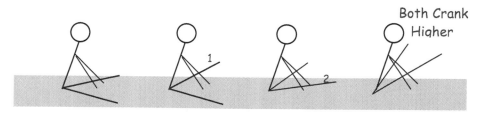

Notes

CONDITIONING AND DRILLS FOR DANCE 2

Renvillations (Advanced Leap Drill)

1. Have your athlete place the heel of one foot on top of a folded mat. This foot remains on the mat throughout the exercise, but it does turn over at one point.
2. Their other leg is behind them as if they are sitting in a split with one foot on a mat and hands supporting them. (Over-Split if possible.)
3. Instruct your athlete to lean forward slightly and lift their back leg off the floor.
4. Once their leg is lifted, instruct them to swing the lifted leg to the side, then forward and above the mat. (Avoid cutting the leg through!)
5. At this point, your gymnast should have the swinging/circling leg in the air in front of their body, toe pointed toward the ceiling, and hands supporting their weight behind them.
6. Both legs should be straight and their feet should be pointed.
7. Make sure your athlete's buttocks does not touch the floor. It should be higher than the mat while their leg is in the air.
8. Keeping that leg in the air and the other foot on the mat, instruct your athlete to quickly turn their body so that the leg in air remains in place, but is now behind and above the body. Your gymnast's belly is facing floor. It should almost represent a scale with their lifted leg.
9. Next, have your athlete swing/circle the same leg to the side again, then forward to land in a split with the back foot/shin on the mat. The same foot has been on the mat the entire time.
10. Once this split is reached, instruct your athlete to lift up their body slightly and turn their hips to face the mat in the starting position, split with front foot on mat.
11. The gymnast's legs must remain perfectly straight throughout this drill. Allow them to make the natural adjustments/cuts with their hands as the leg is circled.
12. Constantly remind your athlete to keep perfect form in order for the drill to produce the correct results...a great leap!

In fond and loving memory of Renville Duncan, our choreographer and so much more...

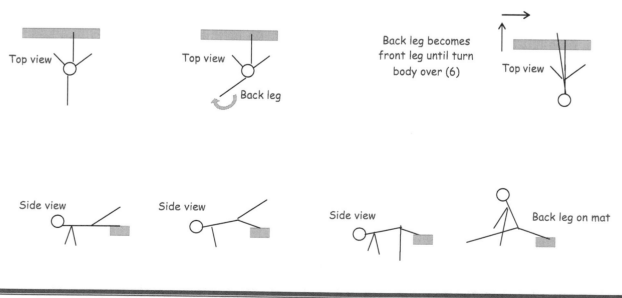

Notes

CONDITIONING AND DRILLS FOR DANCE 3

Lean Back (Advanced Body Tightness Drill)

1. The spotter/coach must be very experienced and strong to spot this drill. It is not possible to do this drill without an extremely good spotter.
2. Place a soft mat behind the athlete in case they become loose and fall.
3. Have your athlete lift their leg so the spotter is holding their ankle.
4. The spotter steps (w/o shoes on) on the athletes foot that remains on the floor in order to prevent the athlete from slipping/falling.
5. The athlete must hold one leg up in front, from their head to the foot on the floor in one straight line, and their arms side/middle.
6. While the athlete remains extremely tight the spotter holds their ankle and lowers them towards the floor. The gymnast's back is facing floor. They are actually leaning back holding a straight body while the spotter is holding one leg.
7. Once the athlete's head comes close to the floor\mat, the spotter raises them back up to the starting position. (standing with one leg in the air)

In fond and loving memory of Renville Duncan, our Choreographer and so much more...

Attitude Leg Lifts

1. Have your athlete sit on the floor with one leg in front of their body, bent at the knee and turned out.
2. Their other leg should be behind their body, bent, and turned out.
3. Your athlete's foot should be directly behind the opposite hip and their knee should be directly behind the hip on same side.
4. Instruct your athlete to sit up tall and lift their front heel and leg several times quickly. Make sure they lift their entire leg as one unit, keeping their ankle and knee even in height throughout the exercise.
5. Next, have your athlete sit tall and lift their back leg several times quickly. Their knee and ankle must lift as one unit, remaining at same height throughout the exercise.

Top view

3

4

Notes

CONDITIONING AND DRILLS FOR DANCE 4

Hanging Swing Splits on Bars

1. Have your athlete hang on a bar without any obstacles in path of their legs.
2. Instruct them to lift their legs up to a split quickly. (one leg at hip height in front of body and the other leg at buttocks height behind the body)
3. Be sure to remind them to remain square.
4. Make sure your athlete's legs do not wander off to the sides. They must keep their legs in line with their hips.
5. Once your gymnast is in the correct position, instruct them to hold the split for a few seconds.
6. Next allow them to bring their legs back down and together.
7. Once your athlete's legs are together, instruct them to lift their legs quickly again, but working the opposite split.

Hanging Switch Leg Drill

1. Have your athlete hang from a bar again.
2. Instruct them to lift their legs up to a split quickly and then switch legs to opposite split position rather than bringing legs down to rest in between splits.
3. Instruct your athlete to remain square (both shoulders and hips same distance from wall they are facing or even with bar) and repeat this exercise several times, but perform one Switch Leg drill at a time.

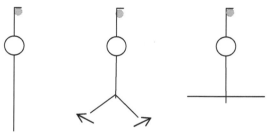

Hanging Hip Flexor Drills - Straddle

1. Have your athlete hang on a low bar without any obstacles in path of legs.
2. Keeping their legs straight, feet pointed, and buttocks under, instruct them to lift both legs so their legs are at hip height. The hanging straddle is the starting position.
3. Next have your athlete lift their legs approximately 6-8 inches higher than hip height and then return to starting position, heels at hip height.
4. Have your athlete repeat this exercise several times quickly. These are mini straddle leg lifts.

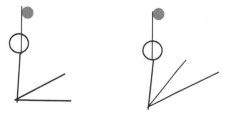

Notes

CONDITIONING AND DRILLS FOR DANCE 5

Hip Flexor (Psoas) Stretch

1. Have your gymnast lie on their back on a mat stack or spotting block.
2. Make sure their buttocks is at the edge.
3. Instruct them to hold one knee close to their chest, with a bent leg.
4. Next instruct your gymnast to lift their other leg above their body with their toes pointed toward the ceiling. This leg can be slightly bent/relaxed. The knee and heel on this leg must be in line with the hip bone.
5. Have your gymnast slowly lower the lifted leg so that it is hanging below the top level of the block or mat stack.
6. Make sure their hanging leg is lined up with their hip and not off to the side.
7. The hip flexor muscles will be slowly stretched while hanging in this position.
8. Your gymnast may wear a light ankle weight, depending upon their level and flexibility.

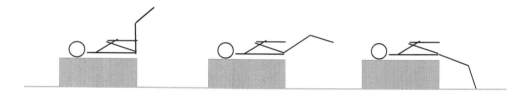

Hip Flexor (Psoas)/Hamstring Stretch

1. Have your gymnast kneel on the floor with one leg in front of their body.
2. Instruct them to shift their weight to their front leg, pushing their hips forward.
3. Once their hips are forward, instruct them to lift their back foot, bending at the knee. Make sure they keep their knee on the floor.
4. Make sure your gymnast's foot is not past their knee for the safest and most efficient stretch.
5. Keeping their feet in place, have your athlete shift their hips back to stretch the front leg's hamstring muscles.
6. Make sure your gymnast is not sitting on their back foot, and that the very top of their thighs are touching each other in order to keep the stretch/ athlete square. Stretching square will help keep your gymnast's splits and leaps square.

Notes

CONDITIONING AND DRILLS FOR DANCE 6

Partner Standing Stretch & Strength (PNF Stretch and Active Flexibility)

1. Lift your gymnast's leg high enough so they feel a stretch in the back of their legs, mostly hamstrings.
2. Make sure your gymnast keeps the supporting leg straight, toe forward, and hips even.
3. Make sure your gymnast keeps the supporting foot flat on the floor.
4. You are stretching them for the first 15 seconds.
5. **After the first 15 seconds** of being stretched, instruct your gymnast **to gently** resist for 10-15 seconds.
6. After the resistance phase, instruct your gymnast to relax and continue to stretch them carefully.
7. Next, hold the heel of your gymnast slightly (1" - 2") lower than the highest stretching point and then instruct them to **lift their leg up** and out of your hand several times quickly. (short leg lifts/kicks)
8. Once your gymnast is able to lift their leg from your hand, have them **lift again and hold** their leg up for as long as possible. (Most gymnasts can only hold this very high leg lift position for only a few seconds in the beginning.)

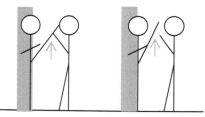

Kneeling Split Stretch

1. Have your gymnast kneel on the floor with one leg in front of their body. Once in that position, stand behind them
2. Next, instruct your gymnast to hold your legs.
3. Once you are both in position, instruct your gymnast to lift the leg forward and up.
4. You will then take hold of hold of your gymnast's leg.
5. Once you have their leg you will slowly pull your gymnast's leg up to stretch them.
6. Press your knees forward enough so that the gymnast does not fall down while being stretched.
7. The supporting leg/knee must remain in one **position** and their hip on the supporting leg side must remain straight and open.
8. Your gymnast's hips must remain square. Do not allow your gymnast to turn the leg in. Make sure their knee faces the ceiling while being stretched.
9. Have your gymnast perform the same resistance and lifting (PNF stretch) as described in the previous stretch after the initial stretching is done.

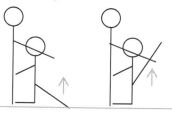

Notes

CONDITIONING AND DRILLS FOR DANCE 7

Form Drills/Leg Extensions

1. Have your gymnast lie on the floor on their stomach.
2. Next have them place their feet on a panel mat or something fairly soft and 8-12 inches high.
3. Instruct another gymnast e who is close in weight to slowly get in a sitting position on the back of your gymnast's knees with their legs crossed and fingertips on the floor for balance.
4. Instruct your gymnast to keep their hips and chin on the floor.
5. Once both are in position, instruct your gymnast to straighten their knees and hold the straight leg position for about 10 seconds.
6. The straight and relaxed movement should be done nonstop until several repetitions are completed.

Leg Curls

1. Have your gymnast kneel on the floor with their hips open and their buttocks off their feet.
2. Next have another gymnast hold your gymnast's ankles to prevent lower leg (shin) from leaving the floor.
3. Instruct your gymnast to lower their body as a unit towards the floor, keeping their hands in front of them to contact the floor as if in the push up position.
4. Once your gymnast is close to the floor they may use her hands (only slightly) to push the floor, but must use their hamstrings to pull them back up to the starting position.
5. Make sure your gymnast's hips remain open throughout the entire exercise. Instruct your gymnast to lead with their shoulders, not their buttocks on the way up.

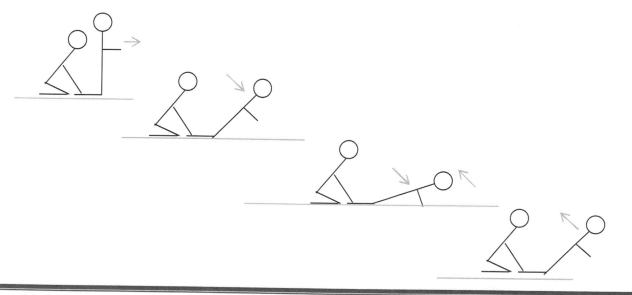

Notes

CONDITIONING AND DRILLS FOR DANCE 8

Kicks (Forward and Back)

1. Have your gymnast stand up straight and tall.
2. Instruct them to quickly lift one leg up high in front of their body.
3. Make sure they kick their toe up rather than out.
4. Make sure your gymnast keeps their legs straight, toe in line with their hip, chest up, back straight, shoulders back, and their hips square.
5. Have your gymnast either return to the starting position or step forward to kick the other leg keeping their legs straight, toe in line with their hip, chest up, and hips square.
6. Make sure your gymnast performs this exercise kicking up and traveling forward and then have them perform this exercise kicking back while traveling forward.

Kick-Kick Bend (Split Leap Drill)

1. Have your gymnast perform the front kick, then lower the same leg/foot and shift their weight to that foot.
2. Next instruct them to immediately kick the other leg up behind their body. As they are performing the back kick, instruct them to simultaneously bend the supporting leg as if they are simulating the proper landing for a leap. It is important for safety and technique that their knee remains in line with their center toe as their knee is bending and straightening rather than leaning inward.
3. Make sure your gymnast keeps their shoulders back and hips square.

Kick-Switch-Bend (Switch Leap Drill)

1. Have your gymnast perform a front kick.
2. Next have them immediately swing the same leg back down and then back to end in a high position behind their body.
3. As their leg is rising behind their body, instruct your gymnast to bend the supporting leg to simulate the landing of a switch leg leap.
4. It is important that your gymnast's knee remain in line with their center toe as their knee is bending and straightening rather than leaning inward.
5. Make sure your gymnast keeps their shoulders back and their hips square.

Notes

CONDITIONING AND DRILLS FOR DANCE 9

Ankle Drills

1. These drills can be done on balance beam with one foot in front of the other (back foot toes touch front foot heel and both turned out slightly. Toes should remain on top surface of the beam.
2. Or this drill can be done on the floor with feet in parallel or facing side on beam and heels below the level of the surface of the beam for an even better stretch.
3. Instruct your gymnast to keep their chest up, buttocks under, and if on beam to remain square.
4. Have your gymnast bend their knees to feel a stretch in their Achilles and ankles.
5. Instruct them to keep their knees bent and lift their heels as high as possible, pushing their feet forward. (forced arch)
6. Keeping their heels high, instruct them to straighten their knees so that they are high on the balls of their feet (releve).
7. Next have them lower their heels to start the exercise again.

Towel Exercises for Arch/Foot Strength

1. Have your gymnast stand with their toes and top portion of their feet on a towel or soft cloth.
2. Instruct them to use their toes to pull the towel so that it ends up crunched under their feet.
3. As your gymnast is pulling the towel with their toes, their arches usually lift so that the gymnast is leaning slightly toward the outer edges of their feet.
4. Once this is mastered, the gymnast can place a small object on the towel in order to add a little weight to the exercise.
5. This usually helps prevent over pronation, the arches of the feet from sagging inward.
6. After performing this exercise for an extended period of time, landings should feel more comfortable and be safer.

Notes

CONDITIONING AND DRILLS FOR DANCE 10

Band Point & Flex (Ankle Strength)

1. Have your gymnast sit on the floor with their legs straight out in front of them, a pike position.
2. Instruct them to place an exercise band around the bottom of their feet and hold the ends of the band with their hands.
3. Next instruct them to point their feet as far away as they can.
4. Once they point their feet as much as possible, they must flex their feet by bringing their toes up and toward their body.
5. Have your gymnast repeat the point and flex positions using the exercise band as resistance for their feet, ankles, and lower legs.

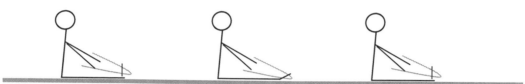

Foot Circles (Ankle Strength)

1. Have your gymnast sit at the end of the balance beam or anything narrow with their heels right at the edge.
2. Next tie an exercise band so that it forms a circle\loop.
3. Instruct your gymnast to wrap the circle\exercise band around the top of both of their feet. The band is around the feet and the feet are at the edge of a beam.
4. Once in place, instruct your gymnast to keep their heels on the beam or narrow table and move their toes outward. Their heels remain in place while their toes make a complete circle outward, down, in, and back up.
5. Have your gymnast continue to circle their toes for several repetitions.
6. After outward circles are performed going out first then down, instruct your gymnast to have their toes go down, out, then back up for a change.
7. Again, have your gymnast perform several repetitions.

Foot Alphabet (Ankle Strength & Stretch)

1. Have your gymnast sit with their legs stretched out in front of them. (pike position)
2. Instruct them to draw the letters of the alphabet in the air with their toes.
3. Their feet should be moving in several different directions as they write each letter, therefore thoroughly stretching and strengthening their ankles.

There is no illustration for this exercise.

Notes

CONDITIONING AND DRILLS FOR PRESS HANDSTAND 1

Seal Press (Abdominal & Upper Body Strength)

1. Have your gymnast lie on the floor, belly down.
2. Next have them place their hands in a pushup position.
3. Instruct them to push up/straighten their arms keeping their hips and legs on the floor. (seal/cobra position)
4. Make sure your gymnast keeps their hands in place, legs straight, and feet pointed (top of feet on floor).
5. Instruct them to slide their feet towards their hands using their abdominal and upper body muscles.
6. Their buttocks should lift/rise towards the ceiling.
7. Next either have your gymnast walk their hands forward and back out to the starting position, or slide their feet out and back down.
8. Other options are to have your gymnast roll out from the top\finish position.
9. You can have them press to a handstand in a tuck, pike, or straddle from the position where their buttocks is at the highest point of the exercise.
10. Instruct your gymnast to perform several repetitions or to travel a certain distance such as down the runway or the floor exercise mat.

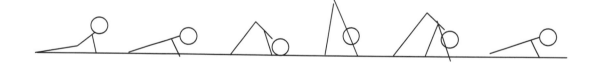

Notes

CONDITIONING AND DRILLS FOR PRESS HANDSTAND 2

Lift Feet, Lift Butt

1. Have your gymnast sit on the floor in a straddle position.
2. Instruct them to place their hands on the floor in front of their body.
3. Have them lift their feet and legs off the floor.
4. While keeping their feet and legs off the floor, instruct them to lift their buttocks up.
5. The goal is to try to lift the buttocks higher than the head, which is the first half of a press handstand.
6. Instruct your gymnast to repeat several times.

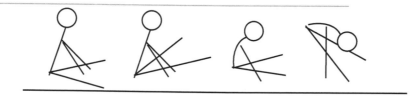

Stalder Roll on Panel

1. Have your gymnast sit on a panel mat in a straddle position.
2. Their feet should be resting on the floor on each side of the mat before they begin.
3. Instruct them to lift their buttocks off the mat and their feet off the floor as if they are performing the Lift Feet/Lift Butt Drill.
4. Instruct your gymnast to press\push down on the mat with their hands, lifting their buttocks.
5. Once their buttocks is high enough, instruct your athlete to roll out on the mat.

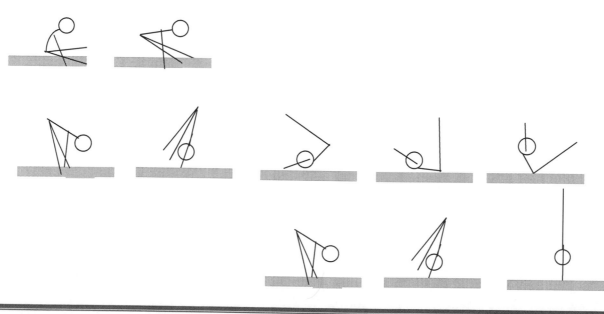

Notes

CONDITIONING AND DRILLS FOR PRESS HANDSTAND 3

Press Lean

1. Have your gymnast stand with their hands flat on the floor in front of their body.
2. Instruct them to position their legs in a straddle.
3. Next have them shift their weight from their feet to their hands. They must then hold their weight on their hands while leaning forward. Your athlete's weight should be on their hands enough for their heels to be lifted completely off the floor.
4. Your gymnast's thighs should be close to their ribs.
5. This will allow them to get comfortable in the pressing position.
6. Make sure your gymnast holds this position at least 10 seconds each time.

Press Lean, Lift One Leg

1. Have your gymnast perform the "Press Lean." While all of their body weight is on their hands, instruct them to lift one leg 4-6 inches from the floor, keeping their thighs close to their ribs.
2. Make sure they hold this position for at least 10 seconds before repeating the exercise with their other leg lifted.

Press Lean Lift to Straddle Through

1. Have your gymnast perform the "Press Lean." While all their body weight is on their hands, instruct them to lift both of their legs approximately six inches from the floor.
2. Once their feet are off the floor, instruct them to straddle through with their legs to finish in a straddle L position. Instruct your gymnast to hold the straddle L position as long as possible.
3. Your gymnast can also press back up half way, similar to the Lift Feet/Lift Butt Drill.

HS Press Through

1. Have your gymnast kick to a straight handstand. (See Handstand Book by Karen Goeller.)
2. Once in the handstand, instruct them to straddle their legs and tuck their buttocks under.
3. Next, have them slowly lower their legs and bring their legs through and forward to a straddle L position.
4. Once they are in the Straddle L position, instruct your gymnast to press back up again, as if performing the Lift Feet/Lift Butt Drill.

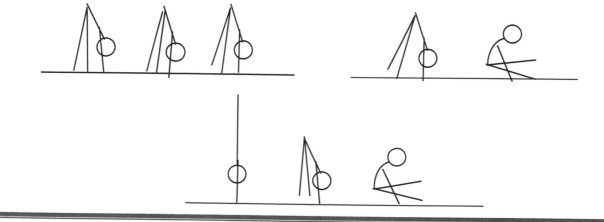

Notes

CONDITIONING AND DRILLS FOR PRESS HANDSTAND 4

Press Lean Feet on Mat

1. Have your gymnast stand with their hands flat on the floor in front of their body. They must be standing in front of a panel mat.
2. Next have them place their feet on a panel mat with their legs in a straddle position.
3. Once in place, instruct your gymnast to shift their weight from their feet to their hands.
4. Make sure they hold their weight on their hands getting comfortable in pressing position.
5. Once comfortable, instruct your gymnast to lean forward even more, bring their thighs close to their ribs, and lift their feet off the mat.
6. Have them straddle wider in the handstand position and bring their feet together over their body to end in a straight handstand.

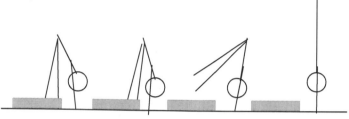

Roll Up Wall

1. Have your gymnast straddle in front of a padded wall and place their hands on the floor so they are in the Press Lean position with their back facing the wall.
2. Your gymnast's hands should be several inches from the wall.
3. Once in place, have them perform the Press and Lean Drill placing their back on the wall.
4. Instruct your gymnast to press their back against wall.
5. Once your gymnast's back is pressing on the wall, have them perform a small roll up the wall and straddle their legs even wider.
6. Once in a straddle handstand, your gymnast can bring their feet together to a straight handstand.
7. Instruct your gymnast to either step down or reverse the exercise by pressing on the wall as they lower their feet to the starting position.

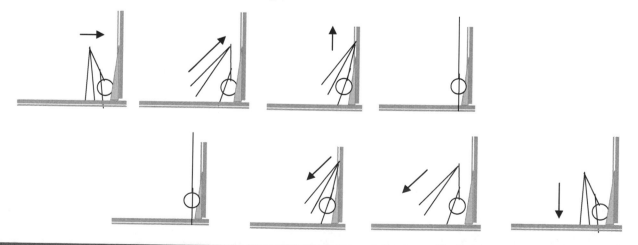

About Karen Goeller

Karen Goeller, CSCS, has educated thousands in the fitness and gymnastics industries with her books, training programs, articles, and in person. She has been training athletes since 1978 and adults since 1985. Karen Goeller is the author of more gymnastics books than anyone in the USA. She is bursting with information that she needs to share with you!

Karen started writing books after she was involved in an accident in 2000 and suffered permanent spinal damage. It was not a gymnastics accident. She stopped coaching gymnastics and left her advertising job. To remain involved in gymnastics and fitness, Karen turned to writing. "I felt like I had a ton of information in my head that was not being used. I knew it was the perfect time to pass on this knowledge and writing books was the perfect avenue."

Karen Goeller's first book, "Over 75 Drills and Conditioning Exercises" was used to create countless successful fitness and gymnastics training programs. Her books have been called the "most useful on the market." Karen's most recent books are the Swing Set Fitness books. They were completed with Brian Dowd, Karen's nephew, who is a physical education teacher. Before the Swing Set Fitness project, Karen's rehabilitation from the accident was slow. It wasn't until the Swing Set Fitness books that Karen started to make good progress. Karen shared, "I finally feel like myself again. I knew I was getting stronger, mentally and physically." When asked if she is healed from the accident, Karen replied, "I am still injured, but that no longer defines me."

Karen has produced State Champions, National TOPS Team Athletes, and Empire State Games Athletes. Three National Champions are from Karen's gymnastics club. All of this success was after her 1991 cancer surgery. The cancer surgery was a success, but Karen was left with lymphedema in her leg and she was forced to keep her leg elevated or in motion 24/7.

Karen Goeller and her athletes have been featured in the media throughout the 1990's including on Good Morning America, GoodDay NY, Eyewitness News, and NY Views (old show) among others. They have also been featured in The NY Times, NY Newsday, Brooklyn Bridge Magazine, and Interview Magazine, and most of the Brooklyn, NY neighborhood newspapers.

More recently Karen was featured on Erin Ley Radio, Lynn Johnson Radio, I Run MY Body Radio, Late Night with Johnny Potenza TV, Talkin' Health with Joe Kasper Radio, the Coast Star, Asbury Park Press, Observer/Reporter, Staten Island Advance, and Inside Gymnastics Magazine.

Karen has worked for world famous Olympic coach, Bela Karolyi and was his first female camp director. Karen also worked at IGC and USAGTC camps.

Before earning her BA Degree, Karen's education included training as an EMT, Physical Therapist, and Nutritionist. She has had certifications such as EMT-D, Nutritional Analysis, Fitness Trainer, many USA Gymnastics certifications, and the NSCA-CSCS certification.

Read more about Karen at www.KarenGoeller.com

Other Books by Karen Goeller

Gymnastics Drills and Conditioning Exercises (Previous edition. 978-1-4116-0579-4)
Over 100 drills and conditioning exercises in this book. Appropriate for developing gymnasts.
Topics: Running, Vault, Bars, Dance, Press Handstand

Handstand Drills and Conditioning Exercises (978-0-615-17724-3).
Topics: Body Tightness, Handstand Shape, Tightness in Motion, Upper Body Strength, Core Strength, and More!

Gymnastics Drills... Walkover, Limber, and Back Handspring (978-1-4116-1160-3)
The walkover drills can be performed to learn the skill or to help maintain flexibility. The back handspring drills are for technique and specific back handspring strength.

Gymnastics Conditioning for the Legs and Ankles (978-1-4116-2033-9)
To improve and maintain lower body strength.

Gymnastics Journal... My Scores, My Goals, My Dreams (978-1-4116-4145-7)
It inspires the gymnast to set goals. There are spaces for scores, goals, meet details, and diary writing.

The Most Frequently Asked Questions about Gymnastics (1-59113-372-6)
Guide for gymnastics parents and competitive gymnasts.

Fitness Journal: My Goals, My Training, My Success (978-1-8472-8444-0)
Record workouts, goals, and meals. Great for people who need motivation or take fitness seriously!

Strength Training Journal (978-1-4357-6265-7)
Record your workouts as you complete them. Great for college athletes, bodybuilders, fitness enthusiasts.

Gymnastics Conditioning Programs: Five Conditioning Workouts (978-0-615-14759-8)
Topics include endurance, core, upper body for uneven bars, and more.

Gymnastics Conditioning: Tumbling Conditioning
Conditioning for twisting, body tightness, upper body strength, plyometrics, and more.

Fitness on a Swing Set! (ISBN: 978-0-6151-4788-8)
Nearly 50 exercises that take place on a playground swing! It's time for a change...

Swing Set Workouts (978-0-6151-5170-0)
Twelve workouts that range in difficulty. They all take place on a playground swing! It's time for a change.

Fitness on a Swing Set with Training Programs (978-0-6151-5028-4)
Nearly 50 exercises and 12 workouts on a playground swing. .

One Swing Set Workout (978-1-4348-1259-9)
One effective exercise routine. It offers the reader a sample of the larger Swing Set Fitness books.

Get these books at www.GymnasticsBooks.com.

Made in the USA
Lexington, KY
11 May 2011

9582555R0